HAL•LEONARD®

VIOLIN
PLAY-ALONG

AUDIO
ACCESS
INCLUDED

PLAYBACK+
Speed • Pitch • Balance • Loop

A NEW MUSICAL
WICKED

D0898702

CONTENTS

2   Dancing Through Life

4   Defying Gravity

6   For Good

8   I Couldn't Be Happier

9   I'm Not That Girl

10   Popular

12   What Is This Feeling?

14   The Wizard and I

To access audio visit:
www.halleonard.com/mylibrary

Enter Code
2320-0552-9650-4076

ISBN 978-1-44950-3001-7

HAL•LEONARD®
CORPORATION
7777 W. BLUEMOUND RD. P.O. BOX 13819 MILWAUKEE, WI 53213

In Australia Contact:
Hal Leonard Australia Pty. Ltd.
4 Lentara Court
Cheltenham, Victoria, 3192 Australia
Email: ausadmin@halleonard.com.au

Visit Hal Leonard Online at
www.halleonard.com

Jon Vriesacker, violin
Audio arrangements by Peter Deneff
Produced and Recorded by Jake Johnson at Paradyme Productions

Dancing Through Life

Music and Lyrics by Stephen Schwartz

Defying Gravity

Music and Lyrics by Stephen Schwartz

For Good
Music and Lyrics by Stephen Schwartz

Slowly, tenderly

I Couldn't Be Happier

Music and Lyrics by Stephen Schwartz

I'm Not That Girl

Music and Lyrics by Stephen Schwartz

Popular

Music and Lyrics by Stephen Schwartz

What Is This Feeling?

Music and Lyrics by Stephen Schwartz

The Wizard and I

Music and Lyrics by Stephen Schwartz